The Arts

PABLO PICASSO

rourke biographies

The Arts

PABLO PICASSO

by
CARL ROLLYSON

Rourke Publications, Inc.
Vero Beach, Florida 32964

For Amelia

∞ The paper used in this book conforms to the American National Standard for Permanence of Paper for Printed Library Materials, Z39.48-1984.

Library of Congress Cataloging-in-Publication Data
Rollyson, Carl E. (Carl Edmund), 1948-
  Pablo Picasso / written by Carl Rollyson.
    p. cm. — (Rourke biographies. The arts)
  Includes bibliographical references and index.
  Summary: Presents the life of Pablo Picasso, from his childhood, through his early artistic efforts, to his world fame as one of the greatest artists of the twentieth century.
  ISBN 0-86625-488-9 (alk. paper)
  1. Picasso, Pablo, 1881-1973—Juvenile literature. 2. Artists—France—Biography—Juvenile literature. [1. Picasso, Pablo, 1881-1973. 2. Artists.] I. Title. II. Series.
N6853.P5R65   1993
709'.2—dc20
[B]   92-44757
                                               CIP
                                               AC

PRINTED IN THE UNITED STATES OF AMERICA

Contents

Color Illustrations

The Arts

PABLO PICASSO

Chapter 1

The Complete Twentieth-Century Artist

No discussion of modern art can be complete without invoking the name of Pablo Picasso, whose career is synonymous with the development of twentieth-century painting, sculpture, and design. A poet and playwright whose works were performed during the German occupation of Paris in World War II, Picasso was as fond of writers as he was of his fellow artists, and he made significant contributions to theater design, book illustration, and ceramics. He helped to define twentieth-century art by constantly shifting his style— catching by surprise and often puzzling even his most ardent admirers.

Picasso could draw objects and figures with superb naturalism, rivaling the beautiful realistic representations of the human figure and face produced by the great Renaissance artists, and he could just as easily paint and sculpt abstract, distorted, and even disfigured objects that were sometimes rejected by the public and critics alike as ugly and valueless as art.

He delighted in amusing his friends with simple pictures drawn on tablecloths and napkins on the same days he was creating human figures with exaggerated features (tiny heads and massive bodies) or with whole new anatomies, with animal faces, eyes positioned on one side of the face, and noses pointing in two directions at once—as if to say that modern art should create its own world and the artist should become his own god, presenting art not as a copy of the

Self-Portrait, *1901*. (AP/Wide World Photos)

universe but as original, intact, and self-sufficient. Why not paint a nose pointing in two directions, since art, unlike life, can show the same thing in several different ways simultaneously?

For Picasso, art could be created with anything: a pencil, a paintbrush, a piece of rope, grains of sand, a clump of clay, a bit of cloth or wire. He was not afraid to experiment, and no material or subject matter was alien to his art. He believed that art could be equal to any situation; that is what makes him the complete artist.

Of course, not every work of Picasso's is a masterpiece, and he scorned people who praised everything he produced. His achievements, however, in so many different media (canvas, metal, paper, and clay) make him the unrivaled master of artistic form. The sheer quantity of his work, beginning in his teenage years and extending into his nineties, has yet to be comprehended. To consider Picasso and his work, then, is to contemplate the particular meanings given to art in the twentieth century.

Tradition and Innovation

One meaning of twentieth-century art inheres in the artist's rebellion against the tradition of representational art, a tradition in which the artist attempts to fashion a work that looks like or "represents" the reality of the thing, scene, or person drawn, painted, or sculpted. Since the Renaissance, artists have tried to make paintings on a flat surface look three dimensional, as if the viewer could walk into the picture because it has depth and volume like real space. In other words, artists attempted to be optically correct and show things in perspective as they appear to the eye, so that objects in the foreground are larger than objects in the background, and the space between objects is measured in proportion to what it would be in "real" life or in a photograph.

Olga Picasso, *1923*. (AP/Wide World Photos)

Influenced by late nineteenth-century painters such as Vincent van Gogh (1853-1890), Paul Gauguin (1848-1903), and, above all, Paul Cézanne (1839-1906), Picasso made painting conform to the artist's inner vision—sometimes flattening perspective as ancient artists did who were not concerned with faithfully recording reality as it actually appeared to the eye but were concerned with their conception of reality, of what was important to the artist and to the community to which the artist belonged. Picasso was not the first but he was the boldest artist to demonstrate that modern art must look beyond the traditions of perspective and of realism; the artist must create a new art, dependent only on the imagination. Such an art would not merely copy the world that already existed, but also it would transform that world and make it beholden to the artist's ideas.

At the same time, Picasso did not abandon the past and tradition; instead he reinterpreted art history and made it more worldly and universal, so that he could simultaneously draw upon various influences—Greek, French, Japanese, and African, for example. Within a single painting, Picasso may employ several styles ranging from the abstract to the naturalistic, which suggests that, in his view, art is a fluid medium, always alive and always open to new notions and innovations.

Style and subject matter are intricately related but are never quite on the same terms with each other from one work to the next. Thus the subject matter (say a human figure) does not dictate the artist's style: a woman's body in a Picasso painting or sculpture can be modeled with great fidelity to human anatomy; that same body can also be taken apart and reassembled to portray a single dominating feature, or the body itself can be so abstracted that only its vague outline can show through layers and layers of geometric, cubed shapes. Whatever Picasso creates is a study of subject, form, and style in itself; he never allows the viewer to forget that there is an artist at work.

Man into Myth

The twentieth century is also the age of biography: more is known about the lives of modern artists, for instance, than was true in any other time. Picasso responded to this fact by making himself into a myth, into the artist who is larger than life—demanding total loyalty from friends, wives, and mistresses, acting imperiously but also sensitively, expressing both his love for and hatred of humanity, his curiosity about the female form and his disgust with it, his sense of solidarity with human beings and his isolation from society, a man and artist who makes up his own rules for art and life—sometimes a cruel man and a brutal artist.

So much is known about Picasso because of his willingness to have his life documented. He allowed one of his mistresses, Dora Maar, to photograph his great painting *Guernica* as he worked on it. At the end of World War II, he invited hundreds of American servicemen into his Paris studio. He befriended many photographers and writers (journalists, poets, and novelists) whom he could count on to support his ideas, magnify his accomplishments, and answer his enemies. He lived and traveled with an entourage as a movie star or a politician might. He oversaw the reproduction of many of his works—particularly the pottery produced late in his career. He took full advantage of his commercial value and became wealthy from his art, yet he never forsook his status as fine artist, always creating for himself as well as for the marketplace.

No other twentieth-century artist has been so successful; certainly no artist has labored harder (Picasso worked almost every day, even when he was depressed or physically ill). His strengths and his weaknesses are those of his age; his contradictions—like the often mismatched planes of his paintings and sculptures—reflect an artist who both registered and sought to dominate the many different elements of his epoch.

Chapter 2

Midnight in Málaga

Picasso loved to embellish the story of his birth: near midnight the midwife had given him up for dead and had turned to comfort his mother, whereupon the doctor (his uncle, Don Salvador) blew cigar smoke in the face of the stillborn baby, who promptly cried himself out of suffocation. Birth can be looked upon as a narrow escape out of a mother's womb, a point of view Picasso would relish given his lifelong mixed feelings about women and about death. Cigar smoke may be harsh, but it gets a man going, and it was all the start needed for this infant prodigy, doted on by an indulgent mother and groomed by a proud father, himself an artist who expected his son to surpass his rather modest achievements.

On December 25, 1884, Spain was rocked by a severe earthquake, the center of which was no more than twenty miles from Málaga. The three-year-old Picasso had to endure six seismic shocks between nine and eleven P.M. Three days later, his first sister, Dolores (known as Lola), was born. These dramatic and disorienting events had an important impact on the highly impressionable young Picasso, who literally could feel the earth open up and see the peace of the familiar world shattered as his father carried him through the streets.

Psychiatrists might suggest—as Alice Miller does in her book, *The Untouched Key: Tracing Childhood Trauma as Creativity and Destructiveness* (1991)—that Picasso relived the trauma of his own birth through the earthquake and his sister's birth, even as his parents spent several days anxiously waiting for the earth to settle down. Miller links the twisted nudes and chaotic landscapes of great paintings such as

Guernica to the artist's earliest suffering. In any case, it seems likely that in his first years Picasso developed a sense of doom that prepared him to respond graphically to the fatal events of the twentieth century.

A Precocious Genius

Embellishing his own legend, Picasso sometimes exaggerated his childhood accomplishments, claiming that his drawing was at once mature and adult-like. (His earliest drawings have not survived.) But he *was* precocious, and given his incredible daily discipline later in life—the hours and hours he spent standing, squatting, and sitting on the floor in front of his canvases, sculptures, drawings, engravings, and ceramics—it is hard not to accept the legend of the infant's continual cry for "piz, piz"—which was short for *lapiz* or pencil, the tool he most often favored as he drew incessantly on paper or in sand spirals resembling a kind of sugar cake (*torruella*) made by pastry cooks in Málaga.

Málaga was a Mediterranean seaport city in the province of Andalusia where Picasso's father, an artist, taught painting and drawing at the School of Arts and Crafts. Málaga's landscape would often appear in Picasso's work, evoking his earliest memories of the strong contrasts described by his friend and biographer, Roland Penrose: "the fertile plain and arid rock, intense light and heat in the open contrasted with the coolness of shaded avenues and the interiors of buildings, the stench of slums with the sweet perfume of tropical flowers, the dust and grime of the earth with the purifying freshness of the sea." This intermingling of urban and rural experiences and of a multitude of clashing sensations perhaps stimulated the artist's later efforts to encompass all of the contrasts of creation in his prolific and diverse work.

Picasso's small but sturdy and compact frame seemed to equip him almost immediately for years of tireless persistence at his art. He had eyes that appeared to devour everything; they were intense and penetrating, and depending on his mood they made him look either fearsome or alive with wit. Roland Penrose insists that Picasso's eyes never lost their deep, intimidating blackness; another biographer, John Richardson, remarks that the artist's fierce gaze, his mirada fuerte, *reflects the Andalusian notion that the staring eye almost literally takes possession of its object. In the case of a woman, Richardson suggests, this "strong gazing" could amount to a case of "ocular rape" and account for the powerful way Picasso took charge of the women and the other things in his life and in his work. What Picasso saw he could draw or cut out of paper almost at once, delighting his childhood companions with quickly assembled representations of people, birds, and animals. His friends liked to watch him put to paper a figure created in one swift continuous pencil line.*

Richardson observes that Picasso had a "typically Andalusian upbringing." He was spoiled not only by his mother but also by a grandmother, two maternal aunts, and several housemaids. Perhaps as a result, throughout his life Picasso craved unqualified affection and tended to take women's attention for granted, while treating them rather contemptuously. The very concept of machismo, Richardson emphasizes, is of Andalusian origin, suggesting that Picasso took it almost as his birthright to dominate women as he dominated his art.

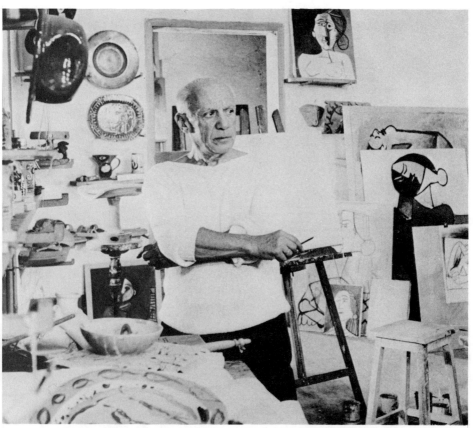

Picasso in his studio in Vallauris, 1953. (AP/Wide World Photos)

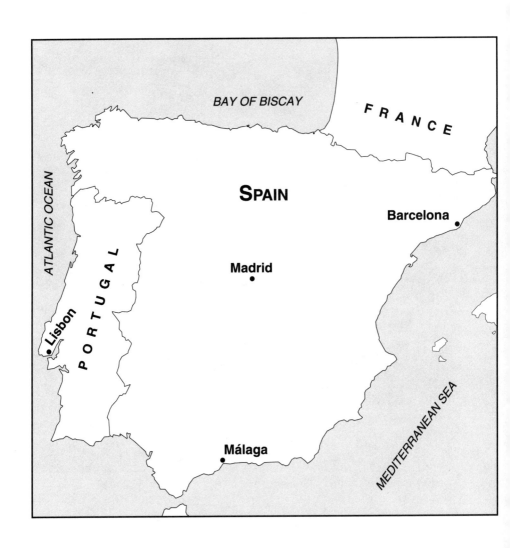

Outside the home, the young Picasso frequented the less prosperous sections of town, where he could observe naked children (up to the age of twelve) running wild in the narrow cobblestone streets and beggars and gypsies delousing themselves. It was there that he learned to smoke with a cigarette up his nostril, to dance a crude flamenco, and other tricks to which he would allude mysteriously in his later years.

Picasso received the conventional training of an art student, learning to draw in charcoal from classical models—plaster casts of Greek heroes and Egyptian goddesses or of legs, arms, ears, and noses, with an occasional stuffed eagle or pigeon. These lifeless models bored the budding artist, who absorbed his lessons quickly and looked constantly for some new stimulus. By the age of ten he was helping his father finish his paintings. The same year (1891), his second sister, Conchita, died—another traumatic event for a young boy who brooded on his own precarious deliverance from death and who would in later years flee from epidemics and other catastrophes that he was sure would overtake him. Three years later he was writing and illustrating his own journals, no longer able to profit from the art schools he attended or even from the instruction of his father, who (legend has it) gravely offered all his colors and brushes to his son, declaring that Picasso had already outdone him and that he would never paint again.

Barcelona

By 1896, the fifteen-year-old Picasso had his own studio in Barcelona, a more cosmopolitan setting for an already accomplished artist frustrated by the academic styles of his day, which emphasized historical subjects and grand depictions of mythological themes far removed from the everyday experience of an active, feisty young man. Not even a move to Madrid, where he qualified for entrance into the Royal Academy, satisfied his restless desire for innovation.

Two years later, recovering from scarlet fever on a trip to the village of Horta de Ebro with a new friend, Manuel Pallarés, Picasso became enchanted with the stone-built houses, the vines and olive trees, the foothills and rustic surroundings, and learned to do everyday country tasks (loading a mule and yoking oxen) that helped him to link his art to nature and to break away from the stuffy traditional subjects for paintings forced upon him by the art schools. Later he would say: "Everything I know, I learned in the village of Pallarés."

The next year, back in Barcelona, Picasso frequented Els Quatre Gats (The Four Cats), a new Parisian-style café and cabaret, meeting avant garde artists and intellectuals (some of them sat for his portraits) and enjoying the first public exhibition of his work. Though he said little in company, he was respected for his precise judgments and his genius, and he managed to make several important friends, who rejected the old-fashioned teaching of the art academies and who explored the urban scene, the city streets, the poor and the downtrodden, looking for subjects in their immediate surroundings and not in history, religion, or the other conventional topics of the day.

Nevertheless, Picasso did not find in Barcelona the major stimulus needed for his work. He seemed convinced of his greatness, calling himself in a portrait *Yo El Rey* (*I the King*), abandoning his father's last name Ruiz and adopting his mother's, declaring an independence that would take him next to Paris, the site of everything that was new in art and that reflected the spirit of social change which the artists of Els Quatre Gats yearned for but could not achieve.

Chapter 3

Paris

The Struggling Artist

In the fall of 1900, having just celebrated his nineteenth birthday and secured permission from his parents (he promised to return by Christmas), Picasso set out for Paris, accompanied by Carles Casagemas, a friend from the Els Quatre Gats days, who supplied some of the money for the trip. Their destination was Montmartre, atop a hill overlooking the city, where several Spanish artists had settled. Picasso and Casagemas divided their time between visiting cafes, dancehalls, museums, and galleries. Thus Picasso was able to observe firsthand the work of important modern artists such as Edgar Degas (1834-1917), Pierre-Auguste Renoir (1841-1919), Vincent van Gogh, and Henri de Toulouse-Lautrec (1864-1901).

As usual, Picasso expressed what he learned almost immediately on canvas, producing *Le Moulin de la Gallette* (1900), a stunning version of Toulouse-Lautrec, evoking the blurred, hazy, interior of a dancehall and a brilliant palette of color. The dancing couples seem to shimmer together as bodies of dark and white light, while in the foreground on the left two women share an intimacy at a table and a woman in front of them smiles, her face more sharply focused as it would be in a photograph of the scene. Also on the upper left, gentlemen in their evening dress enter the dance floor about to merge into the social scene. It is a precise moment, an event, but it is also a tableau, a spatial configuration that allows Picasso to convey both a representation of reality and a unique view of it—in short, an artist's dancehall.

This first brief taste of Paris (Picasso returned home by the end of the year) quickened an appetite for more as the artist became increasingly dissatisfied, finding temporary employment as an illustrator for *Arte Joven* (Young Art) in Madrid and then moving on to Barcelona before realizing in the spring of 1901 that only Paris would do. His first Paris exhibition, given by the art dealer Ambroise Vollard, was a success.

The Blue Period

Despite this initial success, Picasso found that life in Paris was difficult. The money from the paintings he had sold at his first exhibition was quickly spent. Often depressed, hungry, and isolated because he had not yet mastered French, it is not surprising that Picasso turned to melancholy portraits of the urban poor in what has been called his "blue period" (1901-1904).

The Old Guitarist (1903), for example, is suffused with blue as color and mood. The open mouthed skeletal old man is the very image of age and mortality, looking as though he has taken or is about to take his last breath, or has already expired from the exhaustion of his efforts and his years. His right hand hangs limply across the guitar strings while the fingers of his left hand clutch the neck of his instrument which is cradled in his lap. Man and instrument are of a piece; one supports the other. Take away the guitar and the guitarist would surely collapse. The guitar, his art, holds the man together, so to speak, but it is also a part of his poverty. The young, unknown Picasso, who thought of himself as a king in his native land, had to wonder whether he might end up like this fellow artist, all played out.

What is most striking about this early work is Picasso's drawing: the lines of his figures are cut deeply and precisely, almost as if the artist meant to incise his work into the viewer's memory. At about this time Picasso remarked to a friend: "I have no idea whether I am a great painter, but I am a great draftsman."

The most famous work from the blue period is an etching, *The Frugal Meal* (1904), which imparts Picasso's fascination with life stripped to bare essentials. The emaciated, bony, angular figures share a bottle of wine and a small loaf of bread. Shown in profile, the sunken-cheeked man seems blind with suffering and reaches out to his woman, laying his left arm and large bony hand on her left shoulder and placing his right hand with outstretched fingers on her right forearm while she gazes sadly forward (does she provide the blind man's sight?) with her chin resting on her left hand, the fingers contorted— perhaps a sign of her tortured thoughts on the meagerness of a life evoked by her thin, pursed dry lips. Yet however grim, this couple manages a meal, and though they look off in opposite directions, each no doubt enclosed in his or her own suffering, they also form a picture of human solidarity and present one aspect of the human condition, which Picasso is careful neither to sentimentalize nor to ennoble. They represent not a statement but a query—the one Picasso had to put to himself: how does one survive in such squalid circumstances?

The question had taken on some urgency with the suicide of Picasso's friend, Casagemas, in 1901, an event that continued to haunt his early work. Picasso lived a precarious Parisian existence sometimes confining himself to drawing because he could not afford to buy canvas. Befriended by the poet Max Jacob, who admired Picasso's work at the Vollard exhibition, the artist slept in Jacob's bed in a tiny apartment while Jacob worked during the day in a department store. At night Picasso frequented cafes and cabarets and worked. One cold, Parisian winter night, he and Jacob had to burn a pile of his drawings just to keep warm.

Until his fortunes began to rise in the next few years, Picasso would make trips back to his native Spain, taking comfort in his friends and family but also confirming himself in the conviction that he would have to prove and to establish himself in Paris, the only place where he could know for certain the extent of his talent.

Fernande Olivier and the Batteau-Lavoir

In April, 1904, Picasso moved into a dilapidated old studio and apartment building, dubbed the *Batteau-Lavoir* (floating laundry) by Max Jacob, who may have seen a resemblance between it and the barges on the Seine river, where women did their washing. It was very hot in the summer and very cold in the winter, but it provided the room and the company of other struggling artists and writers from whom Picasso would draw inspiration and comfort—clearly a sorely needed environment since he stayed five years, even after he no longer needed to economize.

In the Batteau-Lavoir, Picasso met and fell in love with Fernande Olivier, his first important romantic attachment. Although she was six months younger than Picasso, she had a maturity earned by having left home at seventeen and by suffering through an unhappy marriage. She found Picasso's gaze magnetic yet sometimes disturbing because of its gloomy intensity. Olivier was particularly struck by his contradictions: his intelligence and stubbornness, and his curious way of dressing, wearing at the same time both the clothes of a workman and of an artist, with long hair brushing the collar of a threadbare coat.

The young couple had little money and would resort to various tricks in order to survive, including ordering groceries without immediately paying for them. When the food arrived, Olivier would shout to the delivery boy outside that she was naked and could not open the door. If he would leave it, she

Picasso and friends in his studio in 1944. (AP/Wide World Photos)

would pay later. Some days it was so cold she stayed in bed all day, not having the funds for heating fuel. They had to huddle around a coal stove, their only source of warmth.

Yet the evidence of Picasso's paintings suggests this was not simply a grim, forbidding life. On the contrary, he was happy with Olivier and confident about his art, turning his eye to large painted scenes of circus performers and other nomadic artists who possess a physical mastery and composure but also an aloofness, as if separated from the normal concerns of everyday life.

This is also how Picasso thought of himself, content in his art, following his own hours, staying up very late at night, painting by candlelight, and sleeping until noon. His imagination dispersed the dark, so to speak, and he enjoyed living on the edges of society like the wandering circus performers. After all, as a young boy he had been fascinated with gypsies, a group the budding artist admired for their independence and their ability to create a world apart from the conventions of society.

Of course, this is also exactly what Picasso's poet-comrades would have fostered in him: a disdain for conservative notions of morality, for a 9 to 5 working life, and for all the rules that restricted the artist's imagination. They encouraged Picasso in his search for an art that derived from the streets and roads and fields, and not from what was taught in schools. Picasso had already rejected the art school training of his time which forced students to copy the works of Greece and of the Renaissance and thus curbed their creativity and ability to show what they saw with their own eyes.

The Rose Period

As always, however, Picasso did not merely reject the traditions of the past; he assimilated them into his constant quest for new styles and subject matter. This is especially true in the turn his work took toward the end of the year 1904—sometimes called his "rose" period because the tones of his paintings are no longer blue but various shades of red, brown, and yellow.

Boy Leading a Horse (1906) is typical of this change, for the boy, horse, and landscape are presented in earthy colors but with the stillness of a classical pose, in imitation of Greek statues of young men, perfectly proportioned and composed, presented as ideal versions of humanity. The boy has the stiffness and command of a nude classical figure but his right leg is moving forward in a recognizably country scene. He is not made of marble though his form is sculptural, well rounded, three dimensional and compact—again, all characteristics of classical art, but put in the service of a simple scene that emphasizes the rapport between the boy and the horse, between human and animal natures as the boy guides the moving horse without a rope, its head turned toward his master. The boy, incidentally, has a body similar to the young Picasso's—short and slightly thick in the middle.

By the time Picasso painted *Boy Leading a Horse,* his days as a struggling artist were over, for in 1905 he had attracted the interest of powerful art patrons, especially Leo and Gertrude Stein, who bought his work and wrote about him. Picasso's dealer, Vollard, began to sell his paintings at higher prices, and Picasso's studio became the site for many parties to which writers were invited who would celebrate his genius.

Les Demoiselles d'Avignon

Thus Picasso became known as an artist on the cutting edge, constantly pushing art to its extremes and trying never to repeat himself. Even his closest friends could not always make the shift from one new style to another or did so much too slowly, and the critics often rejected his work, refusing to acknowledge it as art. Curiously, art dealers were more open-minded and continued to buy Picassos no matter how outraged the public, the critical establishment, and Picasso's peers seemed to be. With *Les Demoiselles d'Avignon* (1907), it is almost as if Picasso set up a test case, as if he said to himself, "Now let us see who dares accept this revolutionary painting, the first truly twentieth century work of art."

To this day, the painting continues to puzzle critics, who often resort to explaining it by telling the history of its composition. This is a valid approach, but it tends to deprive the work of its shock value. Look first at the painting: five nude women are shown both frontally and in profile.

On the left the woman with the mask-like face has her left hand raised as if to pull aside a curtain to reveal the other four. The woman in the center raises her arms and tucks them behind her head accentuating the thrust of her breasts. The woman on her left raises her right arm and brings it behind her head while clutching a sheet in her left hand, thus throwing her upper body into a cockeyed diagonal position.

On the right a woman stands with a mask-like face, square shaped breasts, and a snout for a nose. Below her is a squatting woman presented frontally and in profile with a distorted mask-like face and a nose that almost looks like a hatchet. This stylized face has reminded some critics of African masks. The bodies are distorted, sharp edged, with huge rounded eyes found in ancient art, especially in Sumerian sculpture dating back to 3000 B.C.

The woman on the left stands in the stiff, one-foot-forward pose of ancient Egyptian sculpture. Even in profile the eyes are drawn as if they are facing forward, and noses are painted both in profile and as if they too are facing forward—also characteristic of ancient art. Below the women is an arrangement of fruit—probably the last thing that is noticed on a first viewing of the painting.

Les Demoiselles d'Avignon *is shocking for a number of reasons. In the tradition of western art and in much of today's popular culture, a woman's nude figure is usually painted, sculpted, or photographed to appear as pleasing and as uniformly desirable as possible. A naked breast in the movies is always full, round, and melon-shaped, and the rest of the body is perfectly proportioned. This kind of art idealizes women; it also presents a false picture of the way most women look—as Picasso knew from his own early experience of visiting brothels. Not only are Picasso's women not perfectly shaped, they are not inviting, they are not smiling, and they may even be angry or perhaps hiding something. Their feelings are masked, in other words. It is hard to say what they are thinking, and yet they are on display; it may be their reaction to being on display, to being looked at in the nude, that is the subject of the painting. At any rate, the women are definitely holding back something of themselves.*

The painting is also disorienting and shocking because it is not clear exactly where it is set. There is little depth (perspective), and the jagged surface is at one with the uneven edges of the women's bodies. These body shapes are built into the surface of the painting in a manner resembling the cave paintings in France and Spain that date back to 15,000 B.C. Furthermore, again as in cave paintings, it is difficult to say exactly what the figures are meant to represent or what meaning they have for the artist. Neither the painting nor the women are meant to please in the traditional sense of paintings of nude women.

For this reason, Les Demoiselles d'Avignon *can be interpreted as a comment on how twentieth-century art aims to upset our customary expectations of art and of the depiction of the human figure within it. Picasso knew that women are not necessarily pleased with idealization, with living up to the male standards of beauty, with making themselves vulnerable to the male eye. At the same time, his own mixed feelings about women may have contributed to what some would see as the ugliness of the women. Picasso almost always wanted women to give him more of themselves than they were willing to surrender because his demands were tantamount to making them his slaves.*

D'Avignon was a street in Barcelona full of whorehouses, and Picasso knew it well. He also knew that whores play a part, that they pretend to enjoy sex with their customers, and thus are deceiving men, putting on a mask. Sometimes their anger at pretending breaks through the mask; they resent having to offer their bodies like the fruit served up in the bottom center of the painting. Similarly, Picasso did not want to create an art that merely catered to his audience's desires to be seduced; as an artist he did not want to play the whore for his customers.

There is no way to verify this interpretation of the painting, except to say that it has its origins in Picasso's biography and in his knowledge of art history. It is known, for example, that he was beginning to collect African masks and was fascinated with the fact that art in ancient societies was thought to have magical powers. Masks were created both to summon spirits and to banish them. A person could play different roles by donning a mask, just as the artist can become different people by painting them. In other words, the painting itself is a mask of the artist; it gives him permission to explore feelings about the human condition which are not permitted to be expressed in his own person, without a mask. In Picasso's view, art gave him a license to express emotions thought to be impolite or even disgusting in conventional society.

Les Demoiselles d'Avignon caused an uproar. With few exceptions, Picasso's friends condemned it. Henri Matisse (1869-1954), his great rival, thought the painting was a joke or worse. Others predicted Picasso's demise as a great artist. Though Picasso often questioned himself and doubted his achievement, there is no evidence that he wavered during this onslaught on his art. Indeed, he seems to have anticipated it, knowing that the painting would not be understood precisely because it was a breakthrough, like nothing that had appeared before in the history of art. He was preparing himself, in fact, for the next stage of his development: the creation of cubism and his consequent renown as an international artist.

Chapter 4

Cubism and International Renown

Why would artists want to forsake the use of perspective, the brilliant portrayal of the depth and volume of space, which had been developed over five hundred years of European painting? For Picasso was not alone in his quest to create a new art that emphasized not extent of space but the flatness of the picture plane, actually reminding viewers that they are gazing at a picture. Why break and fragment the smooth flow of the Renaissance painter's line?

The answer lies in what has been called the bifurcation of art in the nineteenth century, a splitting of art into two branches: one emphasized realism, making the picture seem as "real," as optically accurate as possible, like the photographs first introduced in the middle of the century; the other championed the artist's independence and vision—the ability, say, to look at a landscape and transform it into a product of the artist's perception.

For Picasso and his generation, the most important artist in this regard was Cézanne. Examine his paintings of Monte Ste-Victoire. The landscape appears not as a realistic photograph but as the deliberately ordered pattern of an artist fascinated with blocks of color, with the soothing greens and warm browns of the land and the cool blues that draw the eye up toward the mountains and the sky.

Cézanne creates a certain form—some might say he reveals an underlying structure in nature—and shows how it can be displayed on a painted canvas. "Look at what he has done with that canvas"—a viewer is just as likely to say this as "Look at what he has done with nature." In either case, however, Cézanne's is an art drawing attention to itself rather than pretending it is merely a window on nature or a mirror of the world.

Picasso aspired to precisely this kind of art: autonomous and self-reflexive; an art, in other words, that refers to itself. Such an art, however, must continue to develop, since it cannot be content with imitating nature. Picasso had to put to himself the question: what happens after Cézanne? In part, he answered his own question by creating *Les Demoiselles d'Avignon,* a painting that began as a naturalistic depiction of a brothel with a sailor who has come to take his pleasure of the naked women.

Gradually the artist destroyed the naturalism of the scene, creating figures, a foreground and a background so intermeshed that there is virtually no depth, only surface, the plane of the picture itself. As a result, the viewer cannot step into the scene; the painting stands almost like a wall and the images within it do not fit into a realistic context. The technique and subject matter of the painting are aggressive and reflect Picasso's insistence on the primacy of his imagination.

Cubism

The next step was to redesign pictorial space altogether, and here Picasso was assisted by a fellow artist, Georges Braque (1882-1963). For almost seven years (until the outbreak of World War I in 1914) the two artists shared an intense partnership, often visiting each other daily, observing, responding, and sometimes elaborating on each other's ideas in what came to be known as their cubist paintings—named as such because they seemed composed of cubes, little square blocks of space, painstakingly built up layer after layer into geometric studies of figures, objects, and landscapes.

Both artists employed a surgical style, dissecting a face, making a huge cylinder out of a nose, squaring an eye, reconstructing a forehead into a diagonal rectangular block, transforming a torso into a network of intersecting triangles, and making the whole body appear as a grand pyramid in granite-gray color—as Picasso did in a portrait of his dealer, Daniel-Henry Kahnweiler (1884-1976).

In cubism, painting became sculptural and architectural in its effects as if canvases had been put together block by block, except that the blocks had a fluidity, a shifting quality that suggested a universe in motion constantly recombining its elements.

There is no single point of view in a cubist painting. The painting itself is a collection, a synthesis of several points of view—suggesting that there are in fact an infinite number of perspectives, not a single perspective as in Renaissance painting.

All points on a cubist canvas are relative: they take their position and importance in relation to each other—in contrast, again, to Renaissance painting, where there is a vanishing point that directs the eye into the painting. Look, for example, at Leonardo Da Vinci's painting *The Last Supper*. The vanishing point is above Christ's head, directing the viewer into and through the scene that is backed with a window at the rear. The illusion created is that of being in a room. It is just this kind of illusion that cubist painting destroys with its many points of view. The cubist painting rejects the notion that there is one way of seeing; it insists there are only ways of seeing, a multiplicity of perspectives.

Picasso and Braque excited each other because they knew they were challenging the principles of art established by the Renaissance. They were engaging in a kind of conspiracy to undermine the complacent notions of art in their time. Yet in their attempts to be analytical, to study space, they were not so different from Leonardo, who did drawing after drawing in order to understand the fundamental structures of nature. On the one hand, Picasso and Braque no longer had the Renaissance confidence that there was a truth, a right point of view; on the other hand, they were bravely exploring what it meant to test the validity of many different ways of looking at the world through art.

They were thoughtful, but they were also playful and hopeful. Art was serious but it was also a game, a competition (in their case) between equals. And they believed art had become an everyday necessity, that it quite literally gave them fresh means of beginning each day. They thought of themselves as inventors, dressed in mechanic's overalls, and Picasso even took to calling Braque "Wilbourg," a variation on Wilbur, one of the Wright brothers who had recently invented the airplane.

Reassembling Reality

In *Still Life with Chair Caning* (1912), Picasso showed what art could do with the everyday. He painted a dissected pipe, a goblet, a lemon, and letters from a newspaper around and on top of a piece of oilcloth, on which the pattern of a chair seat was printed. Instead of a traditional frame, he wrapped the composition with a rope. This is one of the first collages, a kind of composition taken for granted today, in which various separate elements are extracted from their original settings to form a new configuration. The letters

Picasso in a pottery workshop in Vallauris, on the French Riviera in 1948. (AP/Wide
World Photos)

Picasso uses are a pun; in French they begin the words for newspaper (*journal*) and play (*jouer*).

Picasso plays on words because he sees art as play, a game of deception. The chair caning looks real, but it is only cloth. Yet he also sees art soberly; like a journal it is meant to be read, studied, and interpreted. Looking at this painting on the page or on the wall has much the same effect: it is as if we are looking down on it, as if we are above it, as if the items have been placed under a microscope and can suddenly be seen to have a character not visible to the naked or normal eye. This, too, is Picasso's definition of art; cubism allows him to insist that art provides new ways of seeing. And art need not be in a grand frame; it need not be fancy; it can be tied together with a rope.

Cubism tears apart and reassembles things—like Picasso's *Guitar* (1912-1913) made of scraps of wood, cardboard, paper, a tin can, and some wire, and shown from the inside, cut in half. When Picasso did a sculpture of Fernande Olivier, *Head of a Woman* (1909), it became a mass of lumps and blocky surfaces, a head divided into sections, powerful because of its chiseled force. In Picasso's hands, the human form takes on a broken beauty.

New Loves: Eva Gouel and Olga Koklova

By 1911, Picasso's interest in Olivier had waned. She had been the inspiration for several portraits and sculptures, and her worldliness had special appeal for Picasso in the transition he was making between struggling artist and established master, but he was not by nature or by cultural background inclined to remain faithful to any of his women. Approaching thirty, he began the first of what would be a lifelong pattern of liaisons with younger women—all of whom would sooner or later become the subject of his art and help to rejuvenate him during his periods of depression and self-doubt.

41

Picasso called his new love Eva or *My Jolie*, after a song that was popular at the time. Her maiden name was Eva Gouel, but she had invented a new name for herself, Marcelle Humbert, which Picasso rejected, wanting to re-create her in his own terms. Compared to Fernande, Eva seemed youth itself—much younger than the four years that separated them—because she put herself so completely in Picasso's power. Still living with Fernande, he cautioned his intimates not to speak of this new relationship, which he treated as his private treasure. For he enjoyed intrigue and deception, exercising the same absolute control over his love affairs that he had over his art. Rather than making a definite break with Fernande, he simply waited for her to draw her own conclusions, and when she confronted him with the evidence of his infidelity, he simply fled with Eva to another part of the country, ending his seven-year relationship with Fernande.

At the beginning of World War I in August, 1914, Picasso felt isolated. Some of his best friends were enlisting in the army (the bond with Braque would be shattered by his wartime service). Protective of his position as the premier artist of his age, Picasso grew distrustful of younger artists like Juan Gris (1887-1927) whose talent rivaled his. Eva was beginning to succumb to tuberculosis, though Picasso refused to admit it; the nearness of death always frightened him, though he could confront it mercilessly in his art. His biographer John Richardson has observed that in art Picasso was brave; in life he was a moral coward, often taking the easy way out and ducking his responsibilities. He could be quite generous with his peers, but just as often he was spiteful, deliberately disparaging their work.

On December 14, 1915, Eva died. Her early death reminded him of his sister's fate. Gloomy and distraught, Picasso became increasingly difficult to deal with until new interests, a new friend, and a new woman in his life revived him.

Twenty-six-year-old Jean Cocteau (1889-1963) knew how to feed Picasso's genius with flattery and new ideas, feeling it was his destiny to collaborate with a great painter, to entice Picasso into Sergei Diaghilev's (1872-1929) Russian ballet circle, where in collaboration with the composer Erik Satie (1866-1925), they would design, choreograph, and score a new ballet, *Parade*.

For Picasso, this enchanting band was brightened by the presence of Olga Koklova, a Russian ballerina of only moderate talent and beauty but of considerable charm, who yearned for a husband, a home, and family, and who could represent—if Picasso wanted it—the fact that he had arrived and was now a part of the international art establishment. She insisted that he paint her portrait with no tricks; it must be a proper, naturalistically done image of her. That he should readily bow to her desire and portray her in such warm, loving detail is proof enough that he was entering a new phase of life and art.

Paloma Picasso at the Musée Picasso in Paris in 1985. Her father's The Reading of the Letter *(1921) is in the background.* (AP/Wide World Photos)

Chapter 5

The Politics of War and of Art

Parade premiered in Paris in May of 1917. A parody of music hall entertainments (featuring various singing and comedy routines), including four dancers, a Chinese magician, two acrobats, Satie's unconventional score using airplane sounds, a siren, a typewriter, and Picasso's painted curtain with huge cubist figures, *Parade* outraged its audience, which turned against the production in an uproar when a little girl graced the stage riding a bicycle. The traditional decorum of the theater, especially of ballet, had been violated. Guillaume Apollinaire (1880-1918), one of Picasso's poet-confidants, called the ballet an example of "sur-realism," by which he meant a strange intermingling of visual and oral experiences that forced audiences to reexamine reality, to imagine it from a disorienting, intense, and disturbing perspective. *Parade* heralded, in fact, a generation of surrealists in the 1920's and 1930's, perhaps best identified with Salvador Dalí's dreamlike landscapes with cartoonish images seemingly melted and warped—like the watch hanging over a tree in one of his most famous paintings.

It would be a mistake, however, to think of Picasso in these decades as one of the surrealists. Although he shared with them a desire to shake up perceptions of reality, he was not confined to this purpose. On the contrary, from his portrait of Olga Koklova (1917) to *Three Musicians* (1921) to *Family on the Seashore* (1922) to *The Kiss* (1925) it is apparent that his styles shifted back and forth between the naturalistic and the

45

classical, the cubist and the surrealistic. He relished the
opportunity to depict the human body in all of its
voluptuousness, as in *Family on the Seashore,* which seems
inspired by his first happy married years to Olga (their
marriage took place in 1918) and the birth of his son Paolo
(1921). For a brief period, Picasso became a devotee of high
society, far removed from the artist in overalls of the
Batteau-Lavoir days.

Neither Picasso's life nor his art, however, can be easily
confined in categories. By 1925, his marriage showed clear
signs of disintegration—in part because Picasso tired of being
bound by his wife's conventional notions of marriage and of
society, and in part because the artist could not resist the lure
of younger women. In 1927, he met Marie-Thérèse Walter, an
impressionable seventeen-year-old whom he made into his
sexual slave and the subject of a series of pen-and-ink bathing
scenes. Indeed Walter's sensuality seems to have been the
inspiration of many of Picasso's paintings and sculptures in the
1920's and 1930's. *Head of a Woman* (1932) emphasizes in
the nose, the cheeks, and the chin, the rounded, inflated aspects
of the female figure. Similarly, *Woman in Armchair* (1937)
presents his mistress in a spectrum of color, an exotic with
perfectly rounded breasts off to her right like fruits ready to be
picked.

Such paintings and sculptures say as much about Picasso as
they do about his sitter, of course, though his work should not
be reduced to a discussion of his biography. For what Picasso
had to say about men and women in his art is also based on his
keen observation of others and on his responses to culture not
only in his time but also to what artists have revealed in earlier
ages. And how men and women treated each other was
intimately related, in his mind, to the politics of art and of war.
On some level he knew that his contemptuous treatment of
women—not only of Marie-Thérèse but also of his mistress of

Picasso and Jean Cocteau at a bullfight organized by Picasso in Vallauris in 1956.
(AP/Wide World Photos)

the same period, Dora Maar, a talented artist in her own right—was related to the cruelty alive in the world at large that was gradually succumbing to the successes of fascism in the 1930's.

The Art of the Bullfight

Picasso's numerous depictions of bullfights suggest his obsession with blood-rites, ceremonies of violence that expressed humanity's fascination with brutality, even murder, in a manageable form. If there was sadism in the torture of a bull, a love of violence for its own sake, there was also gallantry in the bullfighter's exposure of himself to the raw violence of the bull's charge and art in the attempt to make his confrontation with the bull into a ritual dance. Picasso could work infinite variations on the bullfight in his art as he did in his life, abusing his friends, even taunting them, but also acting gallantly and generously toward them and exerting, in his role as artist, a supreme self-knowledge that did not make him flinch from the cruelty he recognized as a part of his own character.

Art was, in a sense, Picasso's ring, the frame in which he could control and articulate savage emotions, although this did not, unfortunately, prevent him from staging sordid dramas in his own life—such as making Dora Maar and Marie-Thérèse confront each other and fight over him. In *Bullfight: Death of a Torero* (1933) mixed feelings are apparent: anguish over the bullfighter's death, but also a lurid, sexual aggressiveness in the bull's goring of the man's body in an all-devouring, penetrating embrace. The intimacy and totality of the violence that Picasso depicted was shocking but also appealing to a world about to succumb to the irrational and all-encompassing violence of war.

1. *Les Demoiselles d'Avignon*, 1907. (Museum of Modern Art, NY, acquired through the Lillie P. Bliss Bequest)

2. Picasso became identified with Paris, where a museum devoted to his works was opened after his death. (Unicorn Stock Photos/Batt Johnson)

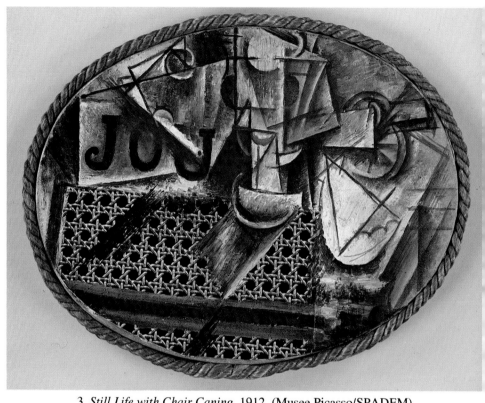

3. *Still Life with Chair Caning*, 1912. (Musee Picasso/SPADEM)

4. *Portrait of Olga Picasso in an Armchair*, 1917. (Musee Picasso/
   SPADEM)

5. *Family on the Seashore*, 1922. (Musee Picasso/SPADEM)

6. *Woman in an Armchair*, 1927. (Musee Picasso/SPADEM)

7. *Bullfight: Death of a Torero*, 1933. (Musee Picasso/SPADEM)

8. The artful violence of the bullfight never lost its fascination for Picasso and can be seen in such works as *Bullfight: Death of a Torero* (preceding) and *Guernica* (following). (Unicorn Stock Photos/Ann Woelfle Bater)

9. *Guernica*, 1937. (Robert Frerck/Odyssey)

10. Velázquez' *Las Meninas*, 1656. (Robert Frerck/Odyssey)

11. *Las Meninas,* 1957. (Art Resource)

12. Picasso was in his eighties when he executed the design for this monumental sculpture in Chicago's civic center, 1966. (Unicorn Stock Photos/Denny Bailly)

Guernica

Picasso's political sympathies were always on the left (he joined the Communist Party in 1944), though his art did not begin to contain explicit political themes until the beginning of the Spanish Civil War (1937), when a group of right-wing military officers, headed by Francisco Franco, attacked the duly elected democratic republic of Spain. Outgunned by Franco and his allies (the fascist regimes of Germany and Italy), the Republic waged a losing battle over a three-year period, gradually relinquishing territory to the rebels, who mercilessly bombed the civilian population.

In early 1937, Picasso had written a poem ridiculing Franco, rejecting his rebellion, treating him as a subhuman type, and evoking the violence of war, the screaming of women, children, animals, of inanimate objects such as beds and chairs and curtains, and of nature itself—a holocaust of screaming that could be seen and smelled because it permeated everything.

Picasso's strongest statement against the assault on the Republic, however, came after the bombing on April 26, 1937, of the Basque capital Guernica. Sixteen hundred of the town's seven thousand inhabitants were killed and 70 percent of the town destroyed by forty-three German bombers and low-flying planes with machine guns.

Working at a furious rate over the course of a month, the artist produced a monumental canvas (twenty-five feet by eleven feet), fulfilling a commission given to him by the Spanish Republic for the Paris International Exposition. The painting was received not merely as a protest against a particular—and particularly horrible—act of war but as a symbol of the irrational forces of terror that had been loosed on humanity in the twentieth century.

The stark brutality of Guernica *is emphasized by Picasso's use of shades of black and white against a rectangular background, creating a field of violence, a killing ground. This mythic scene, expressive of the world's cruelty and not solely the product of a particular evil act, seems timeless, universal. The scene is dominated by the fragmented figures of human beings and animals, arranged both horizontally and vertically—all with mouths open screaming: a man tumbling from a burning building; a woman lamenting the dead baby in her arms; a dead soldier, fallen from his horse, his body in pieces. Another woman dazed by the desolation and chaos is on one knee, her head thrust upward on a diagonal toward the light another screaming woman holds over the soldier. As in so much of Picasso's painting, human faces and bodies are distorted (heads elongated, eyes, hands, and limbs enlarged), shown frontally and in profile at the same time and flattened against the picture plane in order to increase the emotional impact of the setting and the conception of a people, a whole nation suffering.*

Several commentators have remarked that images of the horse and the bull are at the heart of the painting, linking it to Picasso's earlier bullfight paintings employing symbolic evocations of these animals to suggest the power and mobility the artist finds compelling. In Guernica, *the horse is clearly under attack; the bull, however, stands apparently unharmed and impassive, perhaps as an evocation of the impersonal brutality that attracts certain human beings to the bullfight but also of the terrible force the ritual of the bullfight seeks to master.*

At least one critic has interpreted the bull as hovering protectively above the woman wailing over her dead child, though the bull may have more to do with presenting death as part of the ritualistic recurrence of events such as the bullfight and war. In this respect, human beings and animals suffer the same fate. By juxtaposing horse and bull, Picasso seems to acknowledge his identification with the victims while frankly confessing that violence is inherent in the makeup of the universe. It is an austere vision and highly abstract, as befits a painting purporting to encompass the core conflict in the nature of the world and the inevitability of death—so often seen in the human and animal skulls Picasso painted and sculpted before Guernica.

The light bulb shining at the top center and the tile floor of the Paris Exposition visible at the bottom of the painting suggest Picasso's effort to render the horror of war within the confines of art. This is not a naturalistic painting, in which the artist tries to re-create the look and the feel of the actual setting and event or the perspective of an eyewitness; instead the painting offers a highly personal and aesthetic reaction to death and destruction, a deliberate distancing of the artist from the historical facts in order to portray the human condition.

The heavy symbolic load of Guernica *is balanced by the fluidity of Picasso's line, the deftly drawn, flaring nostrils, teeth, and tongue of the horse, the almost equally wide open, concave mouths of the human victims who shout out the vitality of the life that is extinguished. This grim lyricism heightens emotional identification with the lives lost. The expressiveness of the art is at one with the expressiveness of its doomed figures.* Guernica *has been considered one of the finest paintings since Picasso's cubist period because of his power to suffuse the personal symbols and figures of his work with the struggles of a whole people and the fate of twentieth-century civilization.*

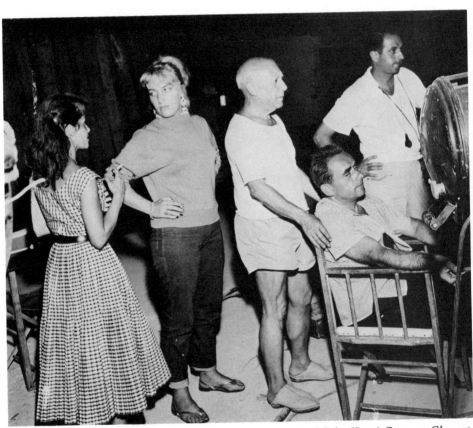

Picasso in 1955 on the set of a documentary film about his life by Henri-Georges Clouzot (seated); at left is Picasso's daughter Maya. (AP/Wide World Photos)

Until *Guernica*, exactly where Picasso stood on the great issues of his time was not understood. It was supposed that he sympathized with leftist and democratic causes, but his art was not interpreted as having a particularly political orientation. In contrast, throughout the 1930's many artists, writers, and musicians explicitly created works that were socially and politically oriented—even directly supportive of political ideologies such as Communism and anarchism.

In *Guernica*, Picasso fused his great reputation with the aspirations not only of the Spanish republic but of all those politically progressive artists and activists who regarded Spain as the testing ground for the defense against fascism. The prestige he lent to the cause of saving Spain can hardly be exaggerated. He had been previously attacked by certain Communist Party ideologues for finding refuge in what they regarded as a solely personal, idiosyncratic, and decadent art that did not reflect the aspirations of the masses or dignify their struggle.

While *Guernica* hardly qualifies as "socialist realism"—the kind of art which the Communist Party saw as faithfully rendering the everyday as well as the heroic actions of the people—there is a sense of collective humanity in the painting that made it possible for Picasso to earn his place on the left as well as maintaining his standing as the foremost artist of his time. In 1939, the Museum of Modern Art gave Picasso his largest retrospective to date, calling it "Picasso: Forty Years of His Art." An exhibition of more than three hundred works, including *Guernica*, it had already been shown to great acclaim in London, Chicago, Los Angeles, and San Francisco.

Picasso ensured his standing among radicals by issuing in pamphlet form a series of etchings called *The Dream and Lie of Franco* (1937), later produced as postcards and sold to raise money for the Republican cause. The image of the aloof artist alienated from his society that had been cultivated in his early

Picasso in his studio after the Allied liberation of Paris in 1944. (AP/Wide World Photos)

period gave way to the artist expressing solidarity with the people, thus ratifying the social and political involvements of many of his contemporaries in art throughout the 1930's. On December 18, 1937, Picasso sent a statement of his political commitment to the American Artists' Congress in New York, affirming that in the attack on Spain the most important values of humanity were at stake. From this point on, he would periodically issue political statements, often drafted by his close communist friends. Picasso would continue his involvement with the Communist Party in the postwar years, attending Party congresses and designing posters for them.

World War II

Guernica was just one of a series of works that Picasso and other artists created in the 1930's that expressed a sense of foreboding, even of apocalypse. The carnage of World War II seemed to confirm these premonitions. Many of Picasso's paintings from the war years have a somber and savage quality, a tone of personal despair best evoked in a series of still-lifes containing the skulls of bulls' heads—the flesh flayed and lit by a naked candle flame.

Picasso's adamant refusal to leave Paris during the German occupation, spurning German offers of fuel to warm his studio and other German gestures that might compromise his opposition to fascism, made the artist a symbol of resistance. In an often told story, he is supposed to have been visited in his studio by a German officer who spotted a photograph of *Guernica* and wanted to know if Picasso had done it. "No," Picasso is supposed to have replied, "You did." There is some doubt about truth of such stories, but Picasso's loyalty to Paris became the stuff of legend, making him into a symbol of freedom and the unvanquished spirit.

Throughout the war, Picasso continued to create chilling renderings of the impact of war on his consciousness.

In Death's Head *(1943), the artist strips away most of the human features from the face, leaving only the rounded hollow eyes and jagged slits for the nose and mouth, suggesting the darkness and hollowness of war at a point when the wrenching emotions of* Guernica *have been spent.*

Similarly, The Charnel House *(1945) goes beyond* Guernica *in presenting war's aftermath, the fact that the earth has become a mortuary, the resting place of the dead, where there is no screaming, where everything has been reduced to a ghastly silence in a world that is just discovering the atrocities of the concentration camps. Instead of the moving figures of* Guernica, *the bodies in* The Charnel House *are tumbled together as in a mass grave with parts of bodies twisted together or gouging into each other, with a frozen gasp of agony expressed on the face of a woman upended and pressing down on the bodies below her. Humanity itself is rent and mangled in this painting.*

Perhaps what is most gruesome about The Charnel House *is that it is not, as in* Guernica, *associated directly with war or with a catastrophic event, for the heap of broken corpses are shown beneath a mundane domestic scene: a white table with an empty jug and an empty saucepan. It is as if the war—not shown on the canvas—has resulted in the bankruptcy of everyday life, which rests upon (or covers up?) a mountain of death.*

Amid the postwar questioning of the very foundations of civilization, Picasso's visions of death and destruction took on new meaning. The Spanish Civil War and World War II were seen not as an aberration, a savage interlude between periods of peace, but rather as evidence of evil strains within civilization itself: a perspective much more frightening than the insight that first prompted Picasso to paint *Guernica*.

Chapter 6

A New Life, a New Art

Picasso never stopped making changes in his life and in his art, searching for ways to renew himself. In part, his quest for innovation reflected the credo of the modern artist who regards himself as constantly overturning the status quo, the customary ways of doing things. In part, Picasso was a restless man—frightened at the prospect of growing old, turning from one mistress to another and younger one, dreading the loss of his physical powers and the onset of death. He worked tirelessly and hoped for another masterpiece to set beside such paintings as *Les Demoiselles d'Avignon* and *Guernica*.

Like most artists who create a great body of work, he produced some pieces that were not particularly good or that merely repeated what he had already done. Because of his enormous reputation, however, Picasso always found a group of friends and critics who praised nearly everything that he did. Although he continued to crave this kind of approval, he was too shrewd not to know that much of his later work did not deserve the highest accolades, and, ultimately, he grew cynical about his friends even as he rejected those who would argue with him or who were less than appreciative of all his artistic efforts.

Françoise Gilot and Jacqueline Roque

It was the same with the women in his life. Françoise Gilot had an independent spirit. Though she moved in with Picasso in 1946, and gave birth to two of his children (Claude in 1947 and Paloma in 1949), their relationship was constantly troubled by her refusal to bend herself to his will—to abase

Picasso with his mistress, François Gilot, and their children, Claude (standing) and Paloma, after a ceremony in which he was made an honorary citizen of Vallauris in 1950. (AP/Wide World Photos)

herself, as Marie-Thérèse had done. And yet when Gilot would leave Picasso, he would come to court her because he found her self-reliant temper such a challenge to conquer. Even when she came back to him, he was frustrated by her aloofness. She was undoubtedly the one woman he was never able fully to master. In one of his rages at her he did an unforgivable thing: he crushed a burning cigarette on her cheek, leaving a scar. Gilot did not flinch.

Such brutality was part of an artist who wanted to mold all matter as an expression of himself. When the canvas failed to yield new art and Picasso suffered dry spells, periods when he could not bring himself to paint, he turned to pottery and sculpture, treating it almost as child's play. *Baboon and Young* (1951), for example, is made out of some discarded pottery, bits of metal, plaster, and two model cars that form its face. The sculpture is, in many senses, about creativity and nurturing: the mother and child, the artist and his materials are joined in the same passionate embrace. Picasso takes the inorganic—essentially dead particles of matter—and reshapes them into a representation not only of life, but of the continuity of life that both mother and child and the artist himself represent.

That Picasso should pick a baboon was not accidental. He loved such creatures and once had a pet monkey, becoming fond of its mischief-making behavior (not so different from the artist's own penchant for pranks), and was persuaded to give up his pet only after it bit him and he was advised that he ran the risk of infection. The threat of illness always scared Picasso, who would literally run away from the first signs of disease and death. Creating art was for him quite literally a means of defying his mortality.

Baboon and Young also reflected the artist's abiding interest in maternity—the loving relationship between mother and child undoubtedly reminded him of his own doting mother,

76

whose love for him was unqualified. Anything less from the
women who loved him drove Picasso to humiliate them and to
demand absolute obedience to his whims.

He was at his tenderest in his art during those periods in his
life when his women gave birth and when his children were
young. He lost interest in his children when they became
adults, and he could treat them as cruelly as he did his former
mistresses and wives. The photographer David Douglas
Duncan, a friend and biographer of Picasso, noted that the
artist was the "most negligent of fathers, whose paternal
interest generally surfaced during school holidays and summer
vacations, when his children's visits to the studio were least
disruptive to his work."

In the mid-1950's, as his relationship with Françoise Gilot
deteriorated, Picasso turned to a new love, Jacqueline Roque,
marrying her in 1961 and making her the subject of several
portraits. She, in turn, became the caretaker of his legend—not
only the last woman he would live with but the one who would
stand by him no matter what. Gradually transforming herself
into the matron of Picasso's house and studio, she screened all
callers and did all she could to amplify and consolidate her
husband's worldwide reputation.

Las Meninas

Picasso, however, was hardly the complacent artist, living
on his laurels and managing his publicity. He enjoyed creating
the mystique of Picasso, but his work always came first, and
he was still capable of producing it in enormous quantities. As
a young man he had been concerned with measuring himself
against the old masters, often imitating their styles and even
signing his paintings with their names.

In old age, Picasso returned to this preoccupation: copying
but also radically transforming the great paintings of Western
art, redesigning them in endless variations as he did in his

forty-four distinct versions of Diego Velázquez' famous work, *Las Meninas* (1656).

Velázquez' *Las Meninas* (*The Maids of Honor*) has sometimes been called the first modern painting. At first glance, it seems to be a picture of various members of the Spanish royal family and their attendants, who are presented in the foreground. To the left of them is the artist, palette in hand, painting them. Behind him in the distant background is a mirror reflecting two figures, perhaps the king and queen, and to the right of the mirror is yet another figure standing in a doorway.

The positioning of these various figures calls into question what the painting is really about. Its first subject may be the maids of honor, but the artist is given almost equal status by standing and, so to speak, commanding the scene by painting it. And he and the maids of honor are being observed by still others who see the scene differently from their individual points of view.

This calling attention to points of view is what is so modern about the painting, for these multiple perspectives imply that what is painted depends on how it is being looked at. The "how" in this painting depends on the artist: it is Velázquez who has chosen not one subject (the maids of honor) but several (everyone who is looking at the maids of honor). Thus Velázquez emphasizes art as a special way of seeing and the artist as a special kind of looker or creator of scenes. It is almost as if he is saying: "Look, this is life as transformed by art." Or "Here is what an artist can make of this scene." Or "Here is a scene dependent on the artist's unique ability to show it from many different angles. What you see depends on where you stand."

That art can show reality or create reality from many different slants appealed to Picasso as the quintessential modern artist, intent on imposing his views of the world through his art, and even more ambitiously, determined to compete with the old masters like Velázquez and to provide new interpretations of their work.

As a modern artist, Picasso took Las Meninas *and pushed it to extremes—in one variation (dated August 17, 1957), he heightened the artist's importance in the scene by having him tower over the court figures by making him twice their size. True also to his belief that art is a matter of multiple interpretations, Picasso bisects the painter's body and gives him two faces in interlocking profiles.*

Velázquez' court scene is dominated by the paintings on the wall, reminding the viewer not only that the scene is being painted by the painter but also that the scene is itself a part of a world of art. In Picasso's version, this court setting becomes instead an artist's studio, with windows opened to give the artist light. By changing the setting, Picasso shifts the burden of the painting's meaning to the artist's milieu, to the confines of his imagination. The painter is no longer attached to his patrons (the king and queen) but is accountable only to his art. It is as if Picasso were saying: This is how a modern painter must alter Velázquez. The modern artist is entirely independent; he chooses his own subject, which derives entirely from his sovereign imagination. He owes nothing to other sovereigns, other kings and queens.

It was characteristic of Picasso not to paint one version of *Las Meninas* but to paint forty-four. Who was to say which version was right, permanent, and not to be altered? If

Velázquez was one of the first artists to experiment with point of view, Picasso was one of the first to say that such experimentation was the very essence of modern art.

However, there is another way to look at Picasso's ceaseless experimentation. He seems to have been uneasy, uncertain when to deem a work completed. Taking on the old masters showed a certain courage, for he was opening himself to comparisons with the greatest artists, but returning to their work in such obvious ways reflected some doubt as well, a prolongation of the artist's technical facility perhaps at the expense of discovering new ideas. In short, did Picasso have anything original to say in art in his last years? Certainly not by comparison with his work up to *Guernica*. But even into his nineties he continued to create with great power, vigor, stamina, and consistency. There is not, in other words, a great falling off in his work. There is no period of Picasso's career that does not deserve careful study and a case-by-case consideration of the quality of his art.

Picasso's variations on *Las Meninas* were of a piece with the paintings of his studio in the 1950's. One in particular, *Jacqueline in the Studio*, fuses the way he viewed his private life and his art. As Ingo Walther observes in *Pablo Picasso* (1986): "There is something rather ambiguous about Jacqueline in this picture: is she really sitting in a wicker chair, or is her head just part of the painting in the background, on an otherwise empty piece of canvas?" To ask such a question is again to point up Picasso's insistence that the artist combines life and art into a new creation, a new environment, which may relate to the externals (to what exists outside the painting) but which is radically transformed by the artist's imagination. In other words, Picasso insists that the world of the painting is one that he has created; he determines the spatial relationships in this world, how people sit and where they are. He is not a copyist of actuality.

Picasso and his long-time companion, Jacqueline Roque, at the Cannes Film Festival shortly before their marriage in 1961. (AP/Wide World Photos)

No modern artist has paid more attention to the tradition of art or has tried to change it as much as Picasso did. He never merely wanted to follow the rules he was taught in art school. The rules were important, and the tradition of art should be respected, but only after the artist has established his own way of creating. In this sense, Picasso is in the romantic tradition, for the romantic artist must assimilate the classics into his or her own sensibility, using only those aspects of the past that can be revitalized.

The problem with the romantic sensibility is that it insists on the artist's ability to grow, adapt, and change continually. It demands the highest level of energy and intensity; consequently, it often exhausts the artist who must spend his passion recklessly and relentlessly. This is what captivated people about Picasso's own person. Until his very last years, he was capable of standing before his canvases, sculptures, drawings, engravings, and ceramics for hour after hour, day after day, almost never breaking his daily routine. This discipline had to carry Picasso past those moments when he did not feel inspired but felt he had to work nevertheless.

Confronting Death

Of course, this kind of obsessive work routine eventually took its toll. In his last years, Picasso began to be dismayed at the deterioration of his health, managing, however, to keep his weaknesses well hidden behind a facade that appeared to be strong—like old stone worn down but still solid. Like many older artists who maintain a facade in public, buoyed up by adulation and intent on keeping up appearances, Picasso would collapse in private, spend days in bed, refuse to see visitors, and indulge in his fears of sickness and death. Even then, however, he had to draw his misery and make of it a thing of his art.

In a series of self-portraits done in the last years of his life

Picasso pictured his horror. In a final self-portrait (June 30, 1972), the artist's gaze is haunted, almost deranged—the right eye dominated by a huge pupil, the left one shrunken to a point, the mouth a tight, straight line, the cheeks sucked in, and the nose dominating the center of the face like the snout of a frightened animal. Lacking flesh, the head is about to make its transition to a skull. It is not, needless to say, a pretty picture. But it is honest and truthful—a tribute, in a way, to an artist who was able to grapple with his own fears and objectify them into art. Nearing the age of ninety-two, Picasso worked until nearly daylight, then died on the morning of April 8, 1973.

Chapter 7

Picasso's Legacy

There is no doubt that Pablo Picasso was the dominant personality among artists in the first half of the twentieth century. He revolutionized not only twentieth-century painting but also the modern conception of the artist. On the one hand, he stood for the rebel, the arrogant individualist, the champion of the avant-garde, the uncompromising innovator. On the other hand, he enjoyed enormous critical and popular success, and his work was accepted as a standard by which subsequent artists would be measured.

To be sure, Picasso had his detractors. There are critics who believe that his best work is to be found in his first two decades as a major artist, which culminated in the great cubist paintings. Even *Guernica* has been treated by skeptics as essentially a repetition of techniques and themes executed with greater freshness and inventiveness in earlier work. Some critics have rejected the cruelty and misogyny of the artist's work and condemned his leering, voyeuristic treatment of women. An honest evaluation of Picasso's career has to grapple with these disturbing elements, though the flaws of the artist and the man do not seem to negate the great truths of his work—not all of which are comfortable or flattering in what they have to say about the human condition. There is a cold, manipulative side to the man and the artist, but also great technical virtuosity and depth of feeling.

Treated as a godlike authority by many of his friends, and deferred to by many critics, collectors, and a large segment of the public, Picasso remained invincible and could easily absorb attacks by those hostile to his art. To this day, he

Picasso in Vallauris, presenting a wall painting for UNESCO headquarters in Paris in 1958. (AP/Wide World Photos)

remains the subject of countless studies and biographies addressed to both popular and academic audiences.

Picasso as Sculptor

Because he worked at sculpture only sporadically, Picasso's achievement in that medium has yet to be fully recognized and evaluated. While it seems fair to say that nothing Picasso produced in painting after 1945 quite matches the genius of his earlier work, it has been suggested that his sculpture after World War II may someday rank with his highest achievements in painting. There is a profound simplicity, ingenuity, and elegance in much of his later sculpture—*Man with Sheep* (1944) and *The Goat* (1950) are good examples. They seem less tortured and worked over than his earlier virtuoso pieces; consequently, they are also more moving because of their fundamental rightness.

Head of a Bull (1943), formed out of the handlebars and saddle of a bicycle, is a kind of joke, but it deftly presents Picasso's idea of art. In a creative act akin to magic, the artist combines inorganic elements to suggest a living thing. What makes this playful construction a work of art? Not technique, but simply the artist's shrewd imagination.

Unlike many artists who reduce the scale and the scope of their work as they approach the end of their careers, Picasso accepted a commission for a Chicago monument in his mid-eighties, a huge metal construction in the civic center that looks like a mythological creature, horselike and yet ethereal, with exposed ribs that allow one to see through its body. It dominates space without blocking the environment. In its spare lines, it is like a drawing come to life. It is a lesson in the way art can adapt itself to public spaces and also have those spaces invade the work of art. In this case, the creature made out of modern metal seems capable of soaring beside the skyscrapers it complements. Almost a childlike, comic creation with its

An engineer's model of Picasso's Bust of a Woman, *for the 110-foot sculpture at the University of South Florida in Tampa, 1972.* (AP/Wide World Photos)

simple, angular lines, it represents a playful, intriguing presence in the urban scene, a welcome interruption of the severe geometry, the blocks and squares, of city life.

Elusive Genius

What was the secret of Picasso's success? There is no simple answer. Like many great artists, he was an excellent promoter of his own work and often made a virtue out of his defects—saying little and measuring his words, for instance, at a time when his knowledge of French was inexact, and thus acquiring a reputation for a kind of laconic wisdom. Picasso knew how to cultivate people—not by flattering them but by communicating his enthusiasms and producing art rapidly, so that he almost always had a body of work to show and to sell. He had a literary sense that appealed to poets who favored self-dramatizing personalities, and he could write poems and plays that enchanted his friends and letters that seduced his lovers.

In an almost primitive, elemental sense Picasso knew how to catch peoples's eyes, to draw or paint or sculpt figures and objects that arrested the attention—even if the viewer did not like them at first glance. With a confidence that awed his friends and critics, Picasso aggressively appropriated the things of this world so that he could transform them into his art.

It is a mistake to divide Picasso's career into too many neat phases. Certainly different periods saw different emphases in his work, but he could easily shift back and forth from naturalistic to abstract styles, from painting to sculpture to pottery and lithography. He liked to absorb new techniques and thought nothing of submitting himself to the teachings of a master potter who might have something unusual to show him.

This is to say that Picasso was not progressing toward some clearly defined goal, some ultimate way to create art. However, he shared with most modern artists a concern with mastering form, with simplifying and analyzing it in almost scientific fashion. Though he was excited by things as they actually looked, his primary mission was not to reproduce them visually but to interpret, conceptually, what the world of objects and figures could mean in painting, in sculpture, in ceramics, on a book page, or on a theater curtain.

The overwhelming quality that is communicated by Picasso's art is his courage. He was never afraid to break new ground, to offend even his closest supporters, and to risk alienating the customers who bought his work. In time, his very contrariness became a part of his myth, and Picassos could be bought precisely because they were unorthodox and uncompromising.

Fruitful Contradictions

Picasso the man is also worth study. He was capable of great generosity and was beloved by many of his friends. Most of them, however, acknowledged a dark side. Picasso could be very hard on anyone who displeased him. He could be devious, cruel, and unreasonable. He would sacrifice anything and anyone for his art in the most ruthless fashion.

How could such an imperfect man create so much great art? Was his work produced in spite of his faults? This seems unlikely, for how could a man blind to his own frailties and moral failings have the honesty required to reveal the world and human nature in his art? On the contrary, because Picasso knew how far short he fell of the ideal, because as an artist he could draw on an immense reserve of self-knowledge, he was able to create complex and sensitive works of art.

This is not to excuse Picasso the man but to point out that art, as he always insisted, inhabits its own world, and the great artist is capable of generating values in the work itself. Detached from his role as creator, Picasso could be as prejudiced and narrow-minded as anyone of his age. But this same man in the grip of the creative act would rise above himself—or, more precisely, scrutinize himself with the talent of an artist. Certainly Picasso learned things from life that he contributed to his art. By the same token, his art took him into a realm that was greater than the sum of the events in his biography.

It seems likely that anyone wanting to understand the nature of twentieth-century art will have to examine the life and career of Picasso. His historical importance is undeniable. Will he also take his place as one of the masters in art history? It would seem so, for his most important works sustain a balance between tradition and innovation, between what is new and what is time-honored in art, and seem to embody an imagination that is at once singular and summative. To look at *Les Demoiselles d'Avignon*, for example, is to look at an art that is simultaneously sophisticated and primitive, an art that calls on the most advanced techniques of the painter and on a fascination with the magical properties of art that extends back to the cave paintings of prehistoric France and Spain. Picasso conceptualized his world, made out of it not only a picture but a point of view, drawing the viewer's eye to his perceptions, and capturing the imagination, therefore, of civilization itself.

Principal Personages

(In Chronological Order)

Ruiz Blasco, Don José : Picasso's father. An artist and teacher in several art academies, his greatest influence on his son came in his early years, encouraging his talent, allowing him to finish paintings Don José had begun, and supporting him in his first years as an independent artist. In his early twenties, Picasso drew away from his father, realizing he could learn nothing more from his academic style, and adopted his mother's family name as his surname, signing himself Picasso rather than Ruiz.

Picasso López, Dona María: Picasso's mother, who not only gave him unqualified affection and unstinting support but also surrounded him in his childhood with other women who doted on him; he became accustomed to demanding absolute loyalty and devotion from his wives and mistresses.

Olivier, Fernande: Picasso's first great love, a shrewd, worldly woman who helped him negotiate his early years in Paris and provided the inspiration for his art. As he grew more successful, she found she could not cope with his growing ego, his interest in other women, and his consequent estrangement from her.

Jacob, Max: A poet, one of many male friends who treated Picasso gener- ously, providing him with an apartment in his early years of struggle, and promoting Picasso's genius in print and at public exhibitions.

Kahnweiler, Daniel-Henry: The subject of one of Picasso's great cubist portraits, an art dealer who championed the artist's work, seeing the greatness of *Les Demoiselles d'Avignon* before any of Picasso's other friends did.

Gouel, Eva (Marcelle Humbert): Four years younger than Fernande Olivier, she replaced Olivier in Picasso's affections. Her death from tuberculosis traumatized Picasso, who had a particular dread of death derived from his youthful shock at the loss of his sister Conchita.

Koklova, Olga: A Russian ballerina who captivated Picasso at a time when he desired a more settled life and a family; he had always been fascinated with Russian culture. She became part of his romance with the theater in the 1920's, when he designed several curtains and stage settings. Ultimately her conventionality bored him, and he turned to younger, more adventurous women.

Walter, Marie-Thérèse: Only seventeen when Picasso met her, she soon was his mistress, while he served as her sexual tutor and confidant. She became the subject of some of his most flamboyant studies of the female figure, and a devoted companion willing to cope with the arbitrary and sometimes cruel behavior of Picasso, her master.

Maar, Dora: A fine artist, she too became caught in Picasso's cruel need to dominate women. His portrait of her, *Weeping Woman* (1937), captures her anguish over their relationship.

Gilot, Françoise: Although she fell under Picasso's spell and gave birth to two of his children, this young artist also exercised considerable independence and eventually left Picasso rather than submit to his increasing need to humiliate women.

Roque, Jacqueline: Picasso's last love, she married the artist in 1961 and became the caretaker of his legend.

Time Line

1881 Pablo Ruiz Picasso born October 25 in Málaga, Spain, first son of Don José Ruiz Blasco (1838-1913) and Dona María Picasso López (1855-1939).

1882 Birth of his first sister, Dolores (Lola).

1887 Birth of his second sister, Concepción (Conchita).

1891 Death of Conchita. Begins helping his father complete his paintings.

1892 Attends art school in Coruna and is taught by his father.

1894 Writes and illustrates his own journals.

1895 Moves to Barcelona and studies at the School of Fine Arts, where his father teaches, and skips elementary classes after taking an examination.

1896 First studio in Barcelona.

1897 Studies in Madrid at the Royal Academy but quits in the winter.

1898 While recovering from scarlet fever, visits the village of Horta de Ebro with his friend Pallarés.

1899 Returns to Barcelona and frequents Els Quatre Gats (The Four Cats); works on newspaper illustrations and etchings.

1900 Shares studio in Barcelona with Casagemas; spends the autumn in Paris painting *Le Moulin de la Galette*; returns to Barcelona by end of year.

1901 Casagemas commits suicide; second trip to Paris; first exhibition at Gallérie Vollard, a notable success; beginning of "blue" period.

1902 Trips back and forth between Paris and Barcelona; shares an apartment in Paris with the poet Max Jacob.

1904 Final move to Paris; establishes studio (Batteau-Lavoir); meets Fernande Olivier, paints *The Frugal Meal*. End of "blue" period.

1905 Meets Leo and Gertrude Stein, powerful art patrons.

1906 "Rose" period; paints *Boy Leading a Horse*.

1907   Paints *Les Demoiselles d'Avignon,* causing an uproar among art patrons and his peers but attracting the attention of the powerful art dealer, Kahnweiler, who becomes his only dealer.

1909   Begins cubist collaboration with Braque.

1910   Completes several cubist portraits, including those of Kahnweiler and Vollard.

1911   First New York exhibitions; meets Eva Gouel.

1912   Leaves Fernande Olivier; *Still Life with Chair Caning.*

1913   *Guitar.*

1914   World War I begins; collaboration with Braque ends.

1915   Eva dies.

1916   Meets Cocteau, Diaghilev, and Satie.

1917   Meets Russian ballet dancer, Olga Koklova.

1918   Marries Olga Koklova.

1921   Birth of a son, Paolo.

1922   *Family on the Seashore.*

1927   Meets Marie-Thérèse Walter.

1932   *Head of a Woman.*

1933   *Bullfight: Death of a Torero.*

1935   Separation from Olga Koklova; Marie-Thérèse gives birth to Picasso's second child, Maya.

1936   Meets Dora Maar.

1937   *Guernica.*

1940   Remains in Paris during the German Occupation.

1943   Meets Françoise Gilot.

1945   *The Charnel House.*

1947   Françoise Gilot gives birth to Picasso's third child, Claude.

1949   Birth of Picasso's fourth child, Paloma.

1951   *Baboon and Young.*

1953   Meets Jacqueline Roque, who becomes the subject of several portraits.

1957   Series of studio pictures, including variations on *Las Meninas.*

1961   Marries Jacqueline Roque.

1972   Draws series of self-portraits.

1973   Dies on April 8.

Selected Works

Title	Date	Type
Study of a Torso, after a Plaster Cast	1894-95	drawing
Self-Portrait	1896	painting
Science and Charity	1897	painting
Le Moulin de la Galette	1900	painting
Self-Portrait	1901	drawing
Self-Portrait	1901	painting
Evocation	1901	painting
The Mourners	1901	painting
The Dwarf Dancer	1901	painting
The Absinthe Drinker	1901	painting
The Blind Man's Meal	1903	painting
The Old Guitarist	1903	painting
Celestina	1903	painting
La Vie	1903	painting
Tragedy	1903	painting
Woman with a Crow	1904	painting
Woman Ironing	1904	painting
The Frugal Meal	1904	etching
Woman in a Chemise	1904	painting
The Actor	1904-05	painting
The Family of Saltimbanques	1905	painting
Salomé	1905	drawing
The Jester	1905	sculpture
Woman with a Fan	1905	painting
Boy Leading a Horse	1906	painting
Gertrude Stein	1906	portrait
La Coiffure	1906	painting
La Toilette	1906	painting
Self-Portrait with a Palette	1906	portrait
Two Nudes	1906	painting
Les Demoiselles d'Avignon	1907	painting

Title	Date	Type
Three Women	1907	painting
Self-Portrait	1907	painting
Nude with Raised Arms	1907	charcoal
Fruit Dish	1908-09	painting
Woman with a Fan	1909	painting
Head of a Woman	1909	sculpture
Factory at Horta	1909	painting
The Reservoir at Horta de Ebro	1909	painting
Ambroise Vollard	1909-10	portrait
Seated Nude	1909-10	painting
Wilhelm Uhde	1910	portrait
Daniel-Henry Kahnweiler	1910	portrait
Girl with a Mandolin	1910	painting
The Accordionist	1911	painting
"Ma Jolie"	1911-12	painting
Still Life with Chair Caning	1912	painting
Violin and Grapes	1912	painting
The Aficionado	1912	painting
Guitar	1912-13	sculpture
Still Life	1914	sculpture
Glass of Absinthe	1914	sculpture
Max Jacob	1915	portrait
Harlequin	1915	painting
Ambroise Vollard	1915	portrait
Olga Picasso in an Armchair	1917	portrait
The Bathers	1918	drawing
Guitar	1919	painting
Serge Diaghilev and Alfred Seligsberg	1919	drawing
Portrait of Igor Stravinsky	1920	drawing
The Rape	1920	painting
Two Seated Women	1920	painting
The Reading of the Letter	1921	painting
Three Women at the Spring	1921	painting
Three Musicians	1921	2 paintings

Title	Date	Type
Family on the Seashore	1922	painting
The Pipes of Pan	1923	painting
Olga Picasso	1923	portrait
Seated Woman	1923	painting
Paulo as Harlequin	1924	portrait
Three Dancers	1925	painting
The Kiss	1925	painting
Paulo as Pierrot	1925	portrait
Studio with Plaster Head	1925	painting
Guitar	1926	sculpture
Woman in an Armchair	1927	painting
Bathers on the Beach	1928	painting
Sculpture	1928	sculpture
Seated Bather	1930	painting
Crucifixion	1930	painting
Painter with Model Knitting	1931	etching
Head of a Woman	1931	sculpture
Girl Before a Mirror	1932	painting
Woman in a Red Armchair	1932	painting
The Dream	1932	painting
Bullfight: Death of a Torero	1933	painting
The Sculptor's Studio	1933-34	46 etchings
Woman with Leaves	1934	sculpture
Minotauromachy	1935	etching
Dora Maar Seated	1937	portrait
Woman in Armchair	1937	painting
Guernica	1937	painting
Bathers with a Toy Boat	1937	painting
The Dream and Lie of Franco	1937	etchings
Night Fishing at Antibes	1939	painting
Woman Dressing Her Hair	1940	painting
Head of D.M.	1941	sculpture
L'Aubade	1942	painting
Still Life with Steer's Skull	1942	painting

Title	Date	Type
Self-Portrait	1943	drawing
First Steps	1943	painting
Death's Head	1943	sculpture
Head of a Bull	1943	sculpture
Portrait of D.M. as a Bird	1943	drawing
Man with Sheep	1944	sculpture
Bacchanal	1944	painting
The Charnel House	1945	painting
Woman-Flower	1946	painting
La Joie de vivre	1946	painting
Françoise	1946	lithograph
Woman Vase	1948	ceramics
The Goat	1950	sculpture
Pregnant Woman	1950	sculpture
Women on the Banks of the Seine, after Courbet	1950	painting
Woman with a Baby Carriage	1950	sculpture
Goat Skull and Bottle	1951	sculpture
Massacre in Korea	1951	painting
Baboon and Young	1951	sculpture
The Crane	1952	sculpture
War	1952	painting
Peace	1952	painting
The Owl	1953	sculpture
Three Doves	1953	ceramics
Model and Monkey Painter	1954	ink and wash
Sylvette	1954	12 portraits
Jacqueline aux Fleurs	1954	painting
Women of Algiers	1955	15 paintings
The Bathers	1956	sculpture
Plate with Bullfight	c. 1957	ceramics
Las Meninas	1957	58 paintings
Female Bather Playing	1958	sculpture
Déjeuners	1960-61	138 drawings

Title	Date	Type
Déjeuners	1960-61	27 paintings
Woman with Outstretched Arms	1961	sculpture
The Chair	1961	sculpture
The Painter and His Model	1963	painting
Head of a Woman	1964	sculpture
Femme couchée au chat	1964	painting
Steel Sculpture	1966	sculpture
The Kiss	1969	painting
The Matador	1970	painting
Bust of a Woman	1972	sculpture

Glossary

Abstract art: Art that does not attempt to represent or copy the way things actually look.

Anarchism: The belief that government excessively restricts human freedom and therefore should be resisted or abolished; more generally, opposition to all forms of authority.

Avant-garde: Artists and thinkers who are at the forefront of their times, creating new styles that challenge tradition; the term is also used as an adjective.

Classical art: Art that is based on the principles of perfect proportion, naturalism, and rationality, first embodied in the art of ancient Greece.

Communism: A political theory based on the teachings of Karl Marx, who envisioned a classless society where the workers would control the means of production; as practiced, for example in Russia and China, an undemocratic system of government in which the power of the ruling Communist Party is absolute.

Cubism: A style of art that broke with the tradition of perspective, dividing the surface of a painting or a work of sculpture into geometric blocks of space.

Decadent art: Art that is judged to be immoral and harmful in its influence according to the standards of a society or a particular religious or cultural group; often such art is subjected to censorship or attempted censorship.

Fascism: An antidemocratic form of government in which power is concentrated in the hands of a dictatorial leader; historical examples include Spain under Francisco Franco, Germany under Adolf Hitler, and Italy under Benito Mussolini.

Modern art: A term used loosely to refer to the various styles and movements that have dominated the art world since the late nineteenth century, when art began to split between optically accurate (photographic) images and impressionistic or abstract images.

Naturalistic art: Art that is highly detailed, attempting to show exactly how things actually look to the eye; more generally, art that is realistic.

Perspective: The technique that makes a painting look three-dimensional, as if it had depth and volume.

Representational art: An imitation of nature, of scenes, figures, and things drawn, painted, or sculpted.

Romantic tradition: An approach to art with roots in the early nineteenth century, rejecting the slavish imitation of classical works and emphasizing the artist's feelings and his or her quest to create something new.

Surrealism: An early twentieth-century art movement, especially influential in France in the 1920's and 1930's, celebrating the irrational and the subversive; the surrealists were particularly interested in dreams and the unconscious.

Bibliography

Beardsley, John. *First Impressions: Picasso*. New York: Abrams, 1991. A clear, introductory study for anyone beginning a study of Picasso's life and art. Describes the most important works and situates both paintings and sculptures in their historical context. Excellent color plates and index.

Besnard-Bernadac, Marie-Laure, Michèle Richet, and Hélène Seckel, eds. *The Picasso Museum, Paris. Paintings, Papiers collés, Picture Reliefs, Sculptures, and Ceramics*. New York: Abrams, 1986. An introduction describing the layout of the museum, a chapter on the artist's personal collection, lists of new acquisitions and exhibitions, a select bibliography, chronology, 871 illustrations, including 58 in full color.

Gilot, Françoise. *Matisse and Picasso*. London: Bloomsbury, 1990. Incisive comments on Picasso's major works in the light of Picasso's friendship and rivalry with his great contemporary. Having lived with Picasso for several years, and as an artist herself, Gilot provides a unique and sensitive reading of his art and its development. Notes and index.

Hilton, Timothy. *Picasso*. London: Thames and Hudson, 1975. More than two hundred illustrations, thirty in color. Chapters on the early paintings, the blue and rose periods, the beginnings of cubism and *Les Demoiselles d'Avignon*, cubism, *Guernica*, and Picasso's last years. Focused more on the work than on the life. Contains detailed bibliographical notes, list of illustrations, and index.

Huffington, Arianna Stassinopoulos. *Picasso: Creator and Destroyer*. New York: Simon & Schuster, 1988. Although Huffington provides very little discussion of Picasso's art, she summarizes reactions to it and analyzes the biographical background of his paintings. Some aspects of this biography are sensationalized, but it does contain important information based on extensive interviews with the artist's friends and associates. Photographs, extensive bibliography, and index.

Penrose, Roland. *Picasso: His Life and Work*. 3d ed. Berkeley: University of California Press, 1981. An extraordinarily detailed discussion of the evolution of Picasso's work. Also contains considerable biographical information, but it is not always reliable or very well integrated into the narrative. Still, this is a valuable source, especially for Penrose's accounts of his firsthand experience with the artist. Notes, bibliography, and index. Copiously illustrated, but most of the reproductions are too small to be of much value.

Richardson, John. *A Life of Picasso: Volume I 1881-1906*. New York: Random House, 1991. Promises to be the best biography of Picasso to date. Authoritative interpretations of the work; shrewd discussions of the life in prose that beautifully integrates art criticism and biography. An insightful chapter on principal sources, informative notes, and index. Superb reproductions, several full-page, half-page, and quarter-page.

Richet, Michèle, ed. *The Picasso Museum, Paris: Drawings, Watercolors, Gouaches, and Pastels*. New York: Abrams, 1989. Chapters on the early work, from *Les Demoiselles d'Avignon* to cubism; the post-World War I period and the theater; the fringe of surrealism; work during the Spanish Civil War and World War II; the decade from 1945 to 1954; and the final years. A list of exhibitions and a select bibliography. Contains 1,840 illustrations, with 41 plates in full color.

Sommer, Robin Langley. *Picasso*. New York: Smithmark, 1988. Sumptuous reproductions of Picasso's paintings and drawings, including a huge foldout of *Guernica* and close-up enlargements of the bull and the horse, a pencil on paper sketch, and a pencil and crayon on paper sketch for the painting. Includes full-page illustration of *The Charnel House*, and many other color plates with accompanying text.

Walther, Ingo E. *Pablo Picasso*. Hohenzollernring, Germany: Benedikt Taschen, 1986. An introductory study, a chapter on Picasso's wartime experience (1937-1945) with two-page layout of *Guernica*, and several black-and-white and color plates of work done during the war, including *The Charnel House*. An informative text with sidebars quoting the artist on various aspects of his work and his attitude toward art. Detailed, illustrated chronology of the life and work and extensive bibliography.

Media Resources

Adato, Perry Miller. *Picasso—A Painter's Diary. The Formative Years*. Film/Video, 35 minutes. *From Cubism to Guernica*. Film/Video, 34 minutes. *A Unity of Variety*. Film/Video, 21 minutes. 1979. Distributed by Coronet/MTI Film and Video. Rare film sequences, unpublished photographs, and interviews with art historians and Picasso's friends cover every period of the artist's life and work, including reenactments of key episodes and voice-overs of Picasso's own words.

Clergue, Lucien. *Picasso: War, Peace, Love*. 51 minutes. 1986. Distributed by Kartes Video Communications. Focuses on the second half of Picasso's career, beginning with *Guernica*, presenting many major works from museums, galleries, and private collections. Also shows Picasso's studios and workplace near Cannes.

King, Edward. *Picasso: The Man and His Work*. Parts I and II. 45 minutes each. 1986. Distributed by Media for the Arts. Created as a screenplay using King's photographs and films to suggest a kind of scrapbook of Picasso's work, tracing its development in chronological order but with flashbacks showing how work in progress was modified. A biographical narrative parallels discussion of the career.

Minkoff, Burton S. *New Ways of Seeing: Picasso, Braque, and the Cubist Revolution*. 58 minutes. 1989. Distributed by Home Vision. Documents an exhibition at the Museum of Modern Art tracing the working relationship between Picasso and Braque, with numerous closeup views and explanations of their most important cubist paintings, interviews with contemporary artists who comment on cubism, and a valuable "behind-the-scenes" look at the way the exhibition was put together.

Musée Picasso. *Picasso: Portrait of an Artist*. 81 minutes. 1989. Distributed by Media for the Arts. Covers the opening of the Musée Picasso in Paris, including the collection the artist assembled for himself.

The Arts

PABLO PICASSO

INDEX